Text: Claire Llewellyn
Consultant: John Stringer B.Sc. (London), M.Ed. (Warwick)
Computer illustrations: Arthur Phillips, Kevin Jones Associates
Watercolor illustrations: Peter Kent
Photo research: Liz Eddison

Editorial Director: Sue Hook
Art Director: Belinda Webster
Production Director: Lorraine Estelle
Editor: Kate Asser
Assistant Editors: Samantha Hilton, Deborah Kespert
Co-editions Editors: Mathew Birch, Robert Sved

U.S. Editorial Team
Editorial Director: Carolyn Jackson
Assistant Editor: Mimi George
Grateful acknowledgment is made to Adele Brodkin and Theron Cole.

Photo credits: Brian and Cherry Alexander: p67 (bottom right); Allsport: p16 (top right), p31 (top); Eric Bach/Britstock-IFA: p85 (top); Trevor Barrett/Bruce Coleman: p18 (bottom left); Andrew Besley/Images: p13 (center); Anthony Blake Photo Library: p48; Alan Carr/Robert Harding: p69 (bottom); Alain Compost/Bruce Coleman: p22; Diaf/Britstock-IFA: p29 (right); Bernd Ducke/Britstock-IFA: p26 (top); Alain Everard/Robert Harding: p27 (top right); The Image Bank: p51 (top, bottom left), p66 (bottom left), p79 (top); Jay/Britstock-IFA: p49 (bottom right), p63 (top right), p81 (bottom right); William Martin/Robert Harding: p10-11; Pictor International: p43; Poguntke/Britstock-IFA: p39 (right); David Redfern/Redferns: p47; Schuster/Robert Harding: p69 (top); Sipa/Britstock-IFA: p13 (top); Westock P. Skinner/Britstock-IFA: p45 (top right); Spectrum: p21 (top right), p28 (top right), p31 (bottom), p84 (top); Frances Stephane/Robert Harding: p66 (top); Tony Stone: p17 (top right), p19 (right), p50, p52 (bottom), p53 (top), p54, p55 (right), p64 (top right), p65, p83 (top); Superstock/Robert Harding: p35 (bottom right); Israel Talby/Robert Harding: p71; Adina Tovy/Robert Harding: p57 (bottom right); Tschariz/Britstock-IFA: p87 (top right); Zefa: p8-9, p13 (bottom), p15 (top right), p22-23, p36 (left), p38-39 (top), p42 (top, bottom), p44 (bottom left), p52 (top), p72 (bottom left), p73 (top right), p82 (top); Zscharnak/Britstock-IFA: p77 (bottom right).

Produced for Scholastic Inc. by Two-Can Publishing Ltd., 346 Old Street, London, EC1V 9NQ, U.K.
Copyright © 1995 by Scholastic Inc. and Two-Can Publishing Ltd.

Library of Congress Cataloguing-in-Publication Data

How things work : Scholastic reference
        p.   cm. — (Scholastic first encyclopedia)
      Includes index.
      ISBN 0-590-47529-0
        1. Technology—Miscellanea—Juvenile literature.   [1. Technology—
Encyclopedias.] I. Scholastic Inc. II. Series.
      T48.H76 1995
      541.3'93—dc20   94-28588
                                               CIP
                                               AC

12 11 10 9 8 7 6 5 4 3 2 1   5 6 7 8 9 0/09

Printed by Proost in Belgium.
Color reproduction by Daylight Colour Art Pte Ltd., Singapore.
First Scholastic printing, April 1995.

How Things Work

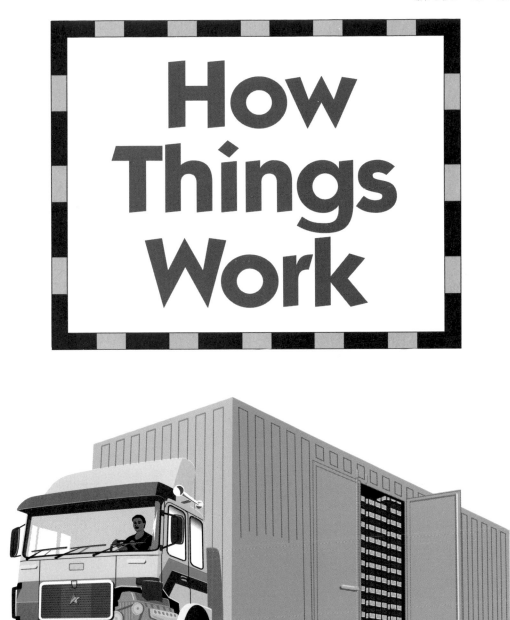

Scholastic
Reference

SCHOLASTIC INC.

New York   Toronto   London   Auckland   Sydney

How to use this book

Look it up!
An encyclopedia (en-SY-clo-PEE-dee-a) is designed so that it is easy to find information. The contents, or entries, in *How Things Work* are organized in alphabetical order. For example, if you want to find out how an airplane works, you will find the entry Airplane near the beginning of the book *How Things Work* because A is the first letter of the alphabet.

Cross-references
Above the colored bar on each page there is a list of other entries in this book or in the other three books in the *Scholastic First Encyclopedia*, with their book titles. These other entries tell you more about the subject on the page. If there are a lot of entries the title of the book only is given. Entries in *A First Atlas* are listed by the map headings. You will find more information in the section that follows the map heading given.

Contents
The Contents page at the front of the book lists the main entries, and which page they are on.

Glossary
Words in the book that may be difficult to understand are marked in **bold**. The Glossary near the back of the book lists these words and explains what they mean.

Index
The Index at the back of the book is a list of everything mentioned in the book, arranged in alphabetical order, with its page number. If an entry is all in *italics*, it means that it is a label on a diagram. If the page number only is in *italics*, the entry appears in the main text as well as being a diagram label.

Pronunciation
Some words, such as encyclopedia at the beginning of the page, are difficult to say. To say them correctly, make the sounds in the parentheses after each of the words. The sounds spelled with all capital letters are pronounced with more stress, or emphasis.

Contents

People and machines	8	Light	50
Machines and movement	10	Metal	52
Airplane	12	Money	54
Bathroom	14	Movie	56
Bike	16	Museum	58
Boat	18	Office	60
Book	20	Oil	62
Bridge	22	Plastic	64
Building	24	Radio	66
Bus	26	Robot	68
Camera	28	Roller coaster	70
Car	30	Space shuttle	72
City	32	Store	74
Clock	34	Telephone	76
Computer	36	Television	78
Electricity	38	Tractor	80
Factory	40	Train	82
Fire	42	Truck	84
Glass	44	Wheel	86
Guitar	46	Glossary	88
Kitchen	48	Index	90

People and machines

How Things Work tells you about the things that people use at work, at home, and at play. It takes things from everyday life and explains how each of them works. It also tells you what goes on behind the scenes in stores and offices, and in the life of a city. The book shows you that many of the things you see around you are made by people.

Making life easier
People have always made tools to help them survive. Early people cut and carved wood to make spears to kill animals for food. Today, most people do not hunt for food, but work to earn the money to buy it at a store. To make their work easier, people often use **machines**.

People working together
Today's work is often complicated. It takes many people working in an organized way to get the job done. Sometimes workers compete to prove they are the best. Other times they work together to reach a goal.

Machines people use

Whether it's an electronic calculator or cash register, a delivery truck or a fork lift, people use machines to make work easier. In factories people even use machines to make other machines.

Machines and movement

There are many different kinds of **machines**. Machines can be simple, like screwdrivers, or complicated, like cars. Complicated machines have hundreds of parts that work together to do a job.

Machines and energy
Just like people, machines need **energy** to do work. This energy can come from many **sources**.

Machines can be powered by people's muscles, by electricity from batteries or **generators** (JEN-er-ay-tors), by fossil **fuels**, such as coal and oil, or by **nuclear energy**.

Forces

Machines need energy to do work. When they are given energy, they begin to work. They change natural **forces** in some way. A screwdriver changes a small force from a hand into a large force that can turn a screw in wood. A car changes the force from moving parts inside the engine into the force that drives the wheels around.

▲ Electricity supplies the energy for this **power shovel** which is able to lift very heavy loads.

Airplane

An airplane is a flying **machine** with wings and engines. It is used to carry goods or people over long distances. The smallest planes seat only one or two people, but huge passenger planes can carry more than 400 people on board. These large planes usually have a crew with a pilot, co-pilot, and flight attendants who look after the passengers.

How a plane flies

Planes can fly because they have wings. If you look at a plane from the side, you will see that the wings have a curved shape. It is this shape that lifts the plane off the ground.

The **streamlined** shape of the airplane allows air to flow past the plane smoothly so that it can fly faster.

airplane rising

air flowing over wing

At take-off, air rushing over the wings creates a **force** called lift. The air below the wings pushes the plane up so that it flies.

Flying is the quickest way to travel. Planes are so fast that on the same day you can have breakfast in London and dinner in New York! Yet traveling by plane is still quite new. The first passenger planes flew not long before your grandparents were born.

Jet engines

Large modern planes are powered by jet engines that burn **fuel**. The engines suck in air at the front, and then blast it out again at the back. The plane shoots forward like a balloon when someone lets the air inside it escape.

Although planes look heavy, they are made of light **materials**, such as aluminum. They stay up in the air because, when they are traveling fast, the lift pushing them up is greater than the weight pulling them down.

▼ Airplanes used in snowy places have skis fitted to their wheels for landing.

▲ The aluminum Lockheed F-117A "Stealth" bomber is covered with a special paint so that it cannot be picked up by **radar**.

At the airport

Each time a plane lands, it is prepared for its next flight by different groups of people. The ground crew makes sure the plane has enough fuel. **Engineers** check many of the plane's electronic control systems. Cleaners clean the passenger cabin and remove the trash. Other staff supply food and drinks to the kitchen.

▲ Cargo is loaded onto a Boeing 747 through its nose. The plane's fuel tank has to carry over 47,000 gallons of fuel.

Bathroom

The bathroom is where you keep yourself clean. It has a sink, a toilet, and usually a bathtub or shower. Water runs to the bathroom along narrow, hidden pipes inside your home. More pipes take dirty water away from the bathroom into a sewer or cesspool. From there it is taken away to be cleaned at a sewage **treatment plant**.

Water and plumbing
Water is usually pumped into homes from the local water system or an underground well. Some water travels along pipes to a tank to be heated up before it is used.

A good flush
As the toilet flushes, clean water pushes the dirty water out. Water in the bottom of the toilet keeps out bad smells from the sewers.

Water on the move

Inside a faucet

When you turn on a faucet, you open a gap which allows the water in the pipe to flow through. When you turn off the faucet, the gap is closed.

on   off

gap

water

1 river

2 pumping station

3 treatment plant

4 storage tower

5 main water pipe

6 home

If you lined up end-to-end all the water pipes used in a two-bedroom apartment, they would be nearly as long as 10 railroad cars.

now picture this

Washing for health

Keeping clean is important for good health. Regular washing gets rid of the invisible **germs** on your body that can make you smell bad and become sick.

Why use shampoo?

The dirt in your hair is greasy and can't be washed out by water alone. A gentle detergent called shampoo loosens the grease, so that you can rinse it away with clean water.

▶ Soap and bubble bath clean your skin in the same way that shampoo cleans your hair.

⑩ river

⑦ sewer

⑧ sewage treatment plant

⑨ clean water

15

Bike

▶ Some racing bikes have wheels made from lightweight carbon fiber. They are very fast.

A bike is a two-wheeled **vehicle** (VEE-hic-el) that both children and adults can ride. Most bikes have no engine. Their **energy** comes from you, as you push the pedals with your feet. Learning to balance on a bike is tricky at first, but it gets easier. When a bike is moving fast, it stops wobbling. This is because the **force** moving the bike forward is stronger than the force pulling the bike down. Once you have learned how to ride a bike, you never forget.

A bicycle

The gears give the bike greater force when you cycle uphill. To work properly, the gears need to be oiled regularly.

ALWAYS WEAR A BICYCLE HELMET TO PROTECT YOUR HEAD IF YOU FALL. MAKE SURE YOU WEAR LIGHT CLOTHES THAT CAN BE EASILY SEEN, ESPECIALLY WHEN BIKING AT NIGHT.

The bike pump pushes air into the tires to give a more comfortable ride.

The chain carries the force from the pedals to the back wheel and makes it turn. It should be well oiled to keep it moving smoothly.

The metal spokes make the wheels strong, but light.

now picture this

Take a bike

Bikes are a very **efficient** (e-FISH-ent) form of transportation. They don't need gasoline or expensive repairs. They are easy to park and are never held up in traffic jams. Best of all, they have no **fumes** to pollute the **environment**.

The longest bike ever built had seats for 35 riders and was over 66 ft long!

The handlebars are for steering.

▲ Bikes are cheap and easy to run. In many countries, bicycles are used as family cars.

The brakes rub against the wheels to slow them down and make them stop. They should be kept clean so that they can grip the tires properly.

The tires have a pattern on them, called the tread. This helps the tire grip the road when it's wet.

Boat

A boat is a **vehicle** (VEE-hic-el) that travels on water. Small boats are used to carry people over rivers and lakes, and along a coast. Larger boats, or ships, cross seas and oceans, but they work in much the same way.

Sink or swim?

Anything will float if it is lighter than water. As long as a boat isn't too heavy for its size, the push of the water upward and inward against it will keep the boat balanced and floating on the water's surface.

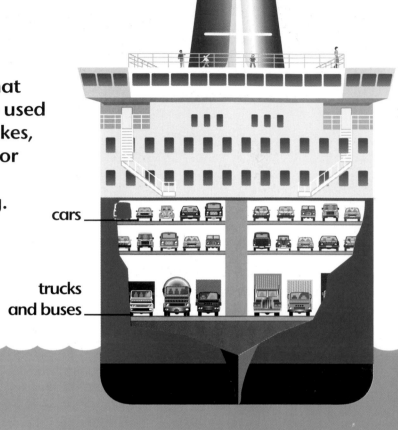

cars

trucks and buses

▲ Vehicles are carefully loaded onto a ferry. Heavy trucks are put low down in the ship to keep the ferry steady in strong winds.

◀ A raft is one of the simplest kinds of boats. It is made of logs that are tied together with rope.

Oil tankers are more than 1,300 feet long. The sailors on them use bikes to get from one end of the deck to the other.

now picture this

Boats in motion

Boats use different kinds of **energy** to move:

Sailboats are driven by the wind. Sometimes there is either too much of it or none at all!

Rowboats have oars to move them through the water. The oars get their **force** from human muscles.

Many boats have engines that turn a **propeller**. With enough **fuel**, they can travel long distances without relying on the wind.

▶ Modern ships are built by joining huge pieces of steel together on a framework.

Some boats are made of light **materials**, such as reeds, **fiberglass**, or aluminum. But modern ships are not light in weight. They are made from heavy metals, such as steel. They stay afloat because of their big, hollow shape. Ships contain so much air that, even though they are so large, they are still lighter than water.

Book

A book is a way of presenting stories, information, and pictures. It contains words printed or written on pages of paper, which are **bound** together in a cover. Different books tell you about different subjects. In a storybook, pictures often help to tell the story. Some books are so popular that they are printed in many different languages.

▲ This book has been printed in Greek, Spanish and English. Only the words have been changed.

Books are produced by publishers. A lot of people work together to make a book. Each person has a different job.

The designer decides how the book will look.

The artist draws the pictures.

The author thinks of the idea for the book and writes the words.

When all the words and pictures are ready, the editor checks that there are no mistakes and sends the book to a printing plant.

Let's say you need 500 copies of a book. At the printing plant, each page of the book is copied 500 times by a **machine** called a printing press. The paper goes from a big roll into one end of the press. The pages come out at the other end. Another machine cuts them and puts them together in the right order.

▶ A big printing press can print many pages together on the same large sheet of paper.

Printing

A printing machine works like a huge rubber stamp although it is more complicated.

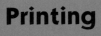

Some computer printers use a **laser beam** to print. Light from the laser burns tiny lines onto special paper. The lines make up the shapes of different letters.

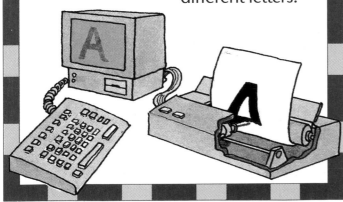

The printed pages are glued, stapled, or sewn together. They are given a stiff hardback cover, which lasts a long time, or a cheaper paperback cover. They go to a warehouse from which they will go to stores, libraries, homes, and schools.

Look in a library!
In a library, books are kept in a special order, so that you can find the title you want. Storybooks are kept in the fiction section. Books with facts, like this encyclopedia (en-SY-clo-PEE-dee-a), are kept in the non-fiction section.

Bridge

A bridge helps people and **vehicles** (VEE-hic-els) cross over a place where roads and paths can't normally go. There are bridges across rivers and valleys, streets, and railroads. On busy highways, bridges called overpasses are built above traffic intersections. These bridges help to keep vehicles moving.

The longest suspension bridge in the world crosses the Humber River in England. It can support 170 big trucks.

now picture this

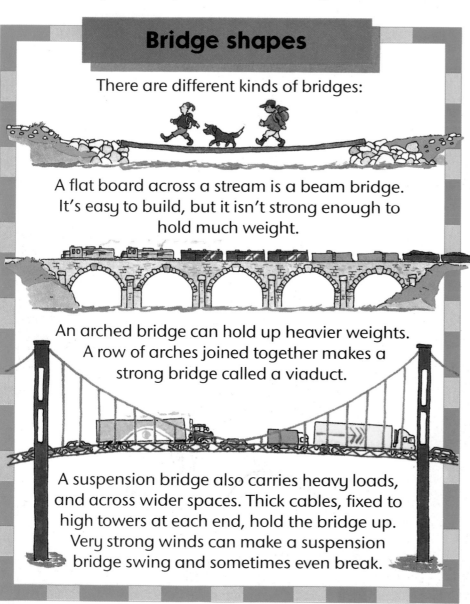

Bridge shapes

There are different kinds of bridges:

A flat board across a stream is a beam bridge. It's easy to build, but it isn't strong enough to hold much weight.

An arched bridge can hold up heavier weights. A row of arches joined together makes a strong bridge called a viaduct.

A suspension bridge also carries heavy loads, and across wider spaces. Thick cables, fixed to high towers at each end, hold the bridge up. Very strong winds can make a suspension bridge swing and sometimes even break.

▶ People first made bridges out of natural materials. This bridge is made from long tree roots that have been woven tightly together.

An **engineer** decides where a bridge should be built and what kind of bridge is needed. The engineer also chooses the best building **materials** for the job. Large bridges are made of strong modern materials, such as concrete and steel. When construction starts, the two ends of the bridge are put in place first. Then the builders work inwards toward the middle.

See also Bathroom, Bridge, Kitchen

Building

A building is a structure with strong walls and a roof. Schools, houses, offices, stores, and factories are all buildings. Buildings can be small rooms or huge skyscrapers. It takes many different people to build a new building, but they don't all work together. Instead they carry out their different jobs in stages.

A new house

1 The architect (ARK-i-tekt) draws up plans of the new house, which the builders will follow.

2 A dump truck brings to the building site the small stones, cement, and sand that are used to make concrete.

4 Builders use **power shovels** to dig ditches for the foundation. The ditches are filled with concrete to stop the building from sinking.

3 Ditches are dug for the gas and water pipes, and for electricity cables.

5 A cement mixer makes the cement that holds the bricks together.

6 Bricklayers build the walls out of bricks or stone blocks cemented together.

7 Carpenters make the roof frame, lay floorboards, and fit the door and window frames.

8 Builders use scaffolding to reach high-up parts of the house.

9 Electricians fit electric wires and cables.

10 Plumbers fit water pipes in bathrooms and kitchens. They also install the central heating pipes.

11 Plasterers smooth the walls with plaster.

Bus

A bus is a large road **vehicle** (VEE-hic-el) with a powerful engine and lots of seats for passengers. Buses carry people around cities and towns, into cities from the countryside, or from one city to another. They are a good, cheap way to get around, especially for people who don't have a car and live far from a railroad or subway. Buses carry lots of people all at once, and help to keep the roads clear.

▲ Many people use buses and streetcars to travel to work in busy cities. Some buses have two decks to carry more people at a time.

A city bus

The bell is used by passengers to tell the driver they want to get off at the next stop.

Some doors open automatically at a bus stop or in an emergency. Others are controlled by the driver.

Taking a bus

Buses run to every part of a city. Passengers find out when the bus runs from a timetable. They wait at the bus stop for the bus, and when it arrives, they pay a fare to travel on it.

The radio allows the driver to keep in touch with the bus company's head office.

As people get on the bus, they pay their fare into a box next to the driver.

▲ In some countries buses are often the only way people can travel to market, unless they walk.

In countries with few cars or fast roads, buses are very important. In the wet season, buses can be the only vehicles able to reach far-away villages along muddy roads. When there are not enough buses to go around, old trucks may be used to transport people as well.

Streetcars

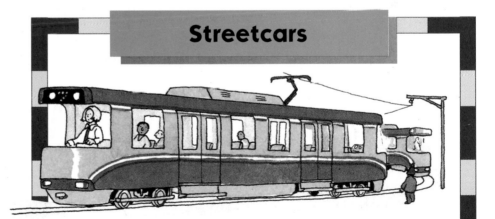

Some cities have electric-powered streetcars instead of buses. A long metal arm on the roof of the streetcar picks up electricity from cables running high above the street.

Camera

A camera is a **machine** that is used to take photographs. The first cameras appeared before the Civil War. The most common kind of modern camera can be carried in your hand and takes photographs that are printed onto paper. Other cameras, such as video and movie cameras, take moving pictures that you watch on a television or at a movie theater.

▶ To keep the camera steady while taking a photograph, photographers can fix the camera to a stand called a tripod.

Taking a photograph

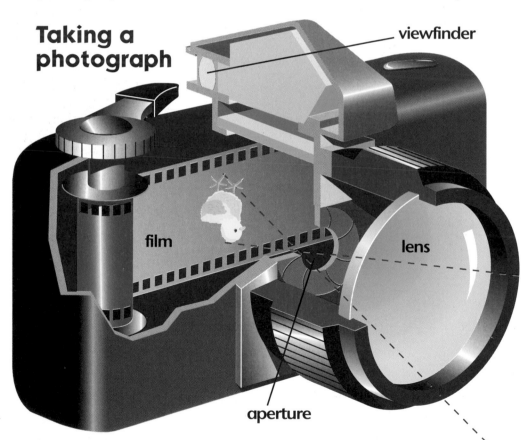

viewfinder

film

lens

aperture

❸ Where the coating of the film is hit by light, it makes a picture.

❶ The viewfinder shows the picture that you are taking.

❷ When you press the button, a hole called the aperture (AP-eh-chur) opens in the camera front. Light shines in through the aperture, and through the **lens**, which directs it onto the film.

Using photographs

People take photographs for different reasons. Family photos help people to remember places that they have visited and the people they've known. Photographs used in newspapers and magazines are not only interesting, but may be better than words at explaining what has happened. Photographs show people what things looked like long ago, or what happened just yesterday.

❹ At a laboratory (LAB-ra-tor-ee), the parts of the film coating without pictures are washed off. A special bath "fixes" the pictures on the film in a strip of **negatives**.

film / photograph

negative

❺ When light is shone through each negative onto special paper, a photograph is made. One negative can make hundreds of pictures.

▲ Underwater cameras have helped scientists to discover much more about life in the ocean.

Moving pictures

Movie cameras take pictures that seem to move. In fact they take many still pictures every second. Your brain "sees" each picture for a short while after it has disappeared. When the pictures are shown quickly one after another, they overlap and seem to join together in a moving scene.

See also Bus, Electricity, Oil

Car

A car is a road **vehicle** (VEE-hic-el) with four wheels and an engine. It is the most popular kind of transportation in the world. If you travel by car you don't have to follow schedules (SKED-jools) or follow bus routes or railroads. Cars have plenty of room for passengers as well as their luggage.

A family car

The steering wheel directs the front wheels.

The ignition key creates sparks that start off explosions that move the car.

The exhaust (ig-ZOST) pipe carries **fumes** out of the engine.

Inside the engine

Cars usually get the **energy** to move from burning gasoline inside their engines. As the gasoline explodes, the **force** of the explosions makes parts of the engine move. As these parts move, they make the wheels turn.

The transmission (trans-MISH-un) gives the car the right amount of **power** to start moving or climb steep hills.

The hand brake and brake pedal work the brake drums.

The brake drum rubs against the wheel to slow it down.

▲ **During a race, the team of mechanics has to refuel a racing car and change its tires in a few seconds.**

Cars old and new

Car fumes are dirty and smelly and pollute the air. **Engineers** have made **filters** to try to solve this problem. A filter is put inside the car's exhaust pipe. The filters clean the dirty fumes as they pass into the air.

Modern cars can go twice as far as old cars on the same amount of gasoline. Some are smaller than old cars and weigh less. A few modern cars do not burn gasoline, but use energy from the sun and other **sources**.

Turn signals warn other drivers that the car is going to turn left or right.

Headlights light up the road for driving at night.

▼ **Cars that run on electricity are clean and quiet.**

A car to suit you

Engineers design cars for different uses. Racing cars are **streamlined** and very fast, but only have room for the driver. Family cars are slower than racing cars, but they have plenty of room for passengers, and don't use as much gasoline. An off-road vehicle is very powerful. Its big tires can cope with the roughest tracks.

City

A city is a large area where thousands or millions of people live and work. To cope with such numbers of people, cities need excellent services. For example, they need plenty of electricity and water, and lots of schools for the children. City life is often fast and noisy, but with movie theaters, museums, stores, and parks, there are lots of things to do.

A modern city

1881

Restaurants serve people dishes from all over the world.

Drains carry water into the sewers.

Gas pipes carry gas into homes and offices for cooking and heating.

Underground subway systems allow people to cross the city quickly.

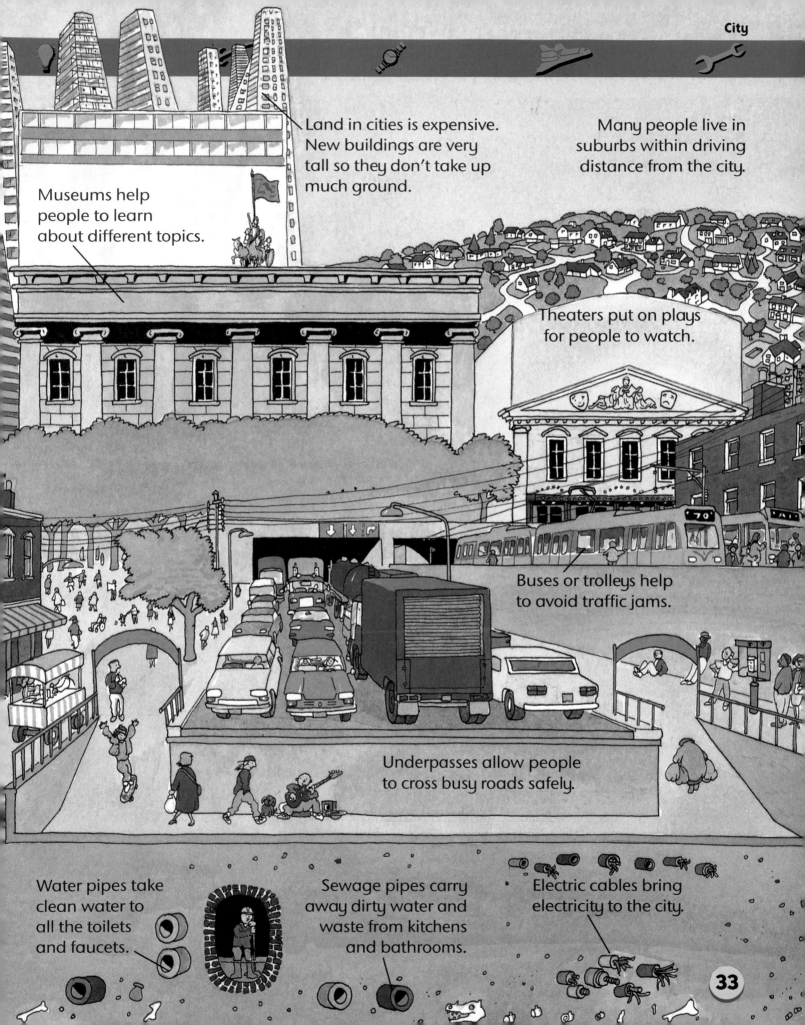

Land in cities is expensive. New buildings are very tall so they don't take up much ground.

Many people live in suburbs within driving distance from the city.

Museums help people to learn about different topics.

Theaters put on plays for people to watch.

Buses or trolleys help to avoid traffic jams.

Underpasses allow people to cross busy roads safely.

Water pipes take clean water to all the toilets and faucets.

Sewage pipes carry away dirty water and waste from kitchens and bathrooms.

Electric cables bring electricity to the city.

33

Clock

A clock measures the passing of time, and tells us what time it is. Some clocks tell the time with two hands that move around a numbered clock face. Digital clocks tell the time with numbers. They are found on stoves or video **machines**. Clocks help us to arrive on time at school, to know when our favorite program is on TV, and to go to bed.

Time around the world

Only half of the earth faces the sun at a single time. When it is midday in one part of the world it is the middle of the night in another. The world is divided up into different time zones, so that all clocks read 12 o'clock when the sun is highest in the sky, wherever the clock is.

Did you know?

Many modern watches will work under water.

The most accurate clock in the world is an atomic clock made in California in 1991. It will lose only one second in 1.7 million years and costs $54,000 to buy.

Before 1687, clocks told the time with only one hand — the hour hand.

▼ These clocks show the time in different parts of the world when it is 9 a.m. in Los Angeles.

9 a.m.
Los Angeles, California

5 p.m. (same day)
London, England

10 p.m. (same day)
Calcutta, India

Clocks with a difference

Hourglasses were invented hundreds of years ago. They used the flow of sand from one half of the glass to the other to measure the passing of time. It took one hour for all the sand to fall through to the other side of the hourglass.

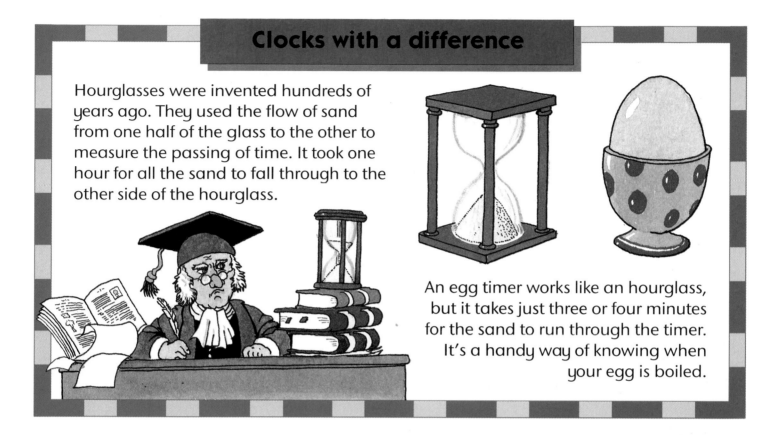

An egg timer works like an hourglass, but it takes just three or four minutes for the sand to run through the timer. It's a handy way of knowing when your egg is boiled.

▶ The Ancient Romans used letters to represent numbers. Some clocks still use Roman numerals to tell the time.

2 a.m. (next day)
Tokyo, Japan

Computer

A computer is a **machine** that works like an electronic brain. It stores much more infomation than most people's brains can, and sorts through it more quickly. However, a computer cannot work by itself. It has to be given instructions to tell it how to do even the simplest job.

A personal computer

Personal computers are small computers that are made for one person to use. Personal computers are found in many offices and schools.

The information in the computer appears on the screen.

◀ Some computers have a hand control, called a scanner, that can read maps. The computer copies the map onto its screen, ready to be used.

The keyboard is like a typewriter. Typing on it feeds information into the computer.

The disk drive is where the computer "reads" information off floppy disks.

Hardware and software

The screen, keyboard, and disk drive of a computer are called computer hardware. The instructions that tell a computer to play a game or write a letter are called the program. Another name for the program is software.

Some computer uses

Engineers use computers when they design new cars. An engineer can make small changes to the design and test them out on the computer screen, without having to build a different model each time.

The police use computers to compare one set of fingerprints with the many thousands of prints they have stored. A computer will find the matching set, if it's there, in just a matter of minutes. Then the police will know who has been at the scene of a crime.

Inside the computer is the hard disk. This is where information is stored and where all the instructions are carried out.

The printer prints information from the computer onto sheets of paper.

The mouse is a small hand control which moves an arrow on the screen.

Information can be stored on a floppy disk. Disks can be carried around and used in different computers.

Electricity

Electricity is a way of moving **energy** around. You can't see electricity, but you can see what it does. It gives us light and heat when we turn it on, and it makes **machines** work. Electricity moves. A lightning flash in the sky is really electricity traveling between clouds and the ground. Electricity is powerful but can also be very dangerous, so we use it with care.

Electricity on the move

❶ Electricity is made in large **power stations**. Most power stations use coal, moving water, or **nuclear energy** to heat water. Steam from the boiling water drives a **generator** (JEN-er-ay-tor).

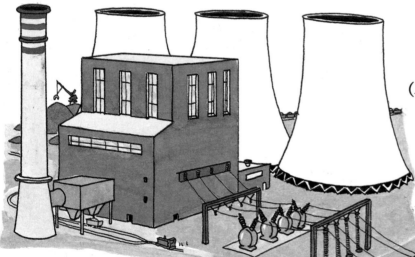

❷ The generator pushes the powerful current along thick wires called cables. The cables are held high above the ground on pylons and carry the electricity to cities and towns.

Electricity flows along special pathways, called circuits (SUR-kits). Most circuits are made from metal wire because electricity will flow through metal. Electricity won't flow through some **materials**, such as plastic, rubber, or wood. Electric wires are covered in plastic or rubber, to make them safe to use. When electricity is moving, we call it an electric current.

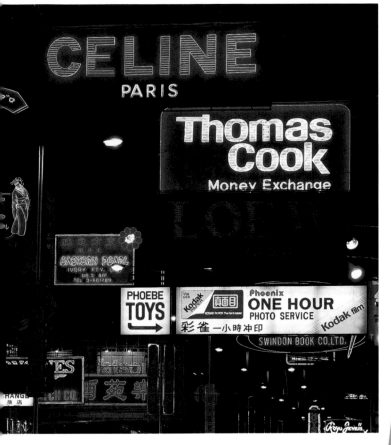

◀ Electric lights allow stores to stay open all night.

Sun and wind

Not all electricity is created at power stations. Smaller amounts of electricity can be produced from natural energy, such as the sun's heat or the wind. Natural **forces** never run out and do not harm the **environment**.

3 In cities and towns, the current is divided into smaller currents which travel along thick underground cables to each street. Other cables branch off of these to carry the current into people's homes.

▲ Wind generators use the force of the wind to make electricity.

ELECTRICITY IS DANGEROUS
ELECTRICITY WILL FLOW THROUGH YOUR BODY. IF YOU TOUCH A BARE WIRE OR A SOCKET THAT HAS ELECTRICITY FLOWING THROUGH IT, YOU WILL GET AN ELECTRIC SHOCK. THIS COULD KILL YOU.

Factory

A factory is a building where things are made. Most of the things we buy, such as cars, clothes, and washing **machines**, are made in large numbers in factories. Factories can buy huge amounts of the **materials** they need, at the lowest possible prices. They use machines, which are operated by people or robots, to make the goods. **Mass production** is the cheapest way of making goods. That is why few things are made by hand today.

Inside a bike factory

❶ Metal tubing for the bike frame is delivered to the factory.

❻ Machines clean and paint the frames.

❼ Some tricky parts of the bike frame are made by hand.

❽ The small parts of the bike, such as brakes and gears, are stored in one part of the factory.

❾ The small parts are fitted to the bike one at a time.

2 Sawing machines cut the tubing into different lengths.

3 Wire brushes rub the ends of the tubing smooth.

5 Robots join the tubing together to make the bike frame.

4 Other machines shape the tubing.

11 The wheels and seat are added to the bike.

10 The wheel spokes and tires are fitted to the wheels.

12 The bike is taken to the **distribution warehouse.**

41

Fire

Fire is the hot, bright flame that is made when something burns. It gives off both heat and light, as well as smoke. If you have sat by a campfire, you know how bright and warm a fire can be. People discovered fire nearly two million years ago. They found that if they hit together two pieces of hard flint stone, they could make a spark. If the spark landed on dry grass, it started a fire. To keep the fire burning, they needed **fuel** such as wood or coal, and air.

▲ When air is heated by fire, it rises. This is how a hot-air balloon works.

Fire for cooking

Controlled fire is very useful. People have learned to use fire for heating and cooking food. A gentle flame can make soup warm. A hot oven cooks a lump of soft dough so it becomes a crunchy cookie.

Fire in factories

Fire is used in factories to make many kinds of things. The fire of a hot furnace melts metal until it can be hammered into different shapes. A kiln is a kind of oven that uses fire to cook clay pots or bricks to make them hard.

▲ When fireworks are set off each one may become nearly 40 times as hot as steam from a boiling kettle.

Emergency!
Fires can also be very dangerous. Every town and city has a department of people who are trained to fight fires. Firefighters wear special equipment to protect them from the smoke and flames. They wear masks to keep their lungs from filling with smoke. Even with this protection, the work is still dangerous.

Glass

Glass is a hard, breakable **material** that is see-through. It may be flat, as for window panes, or it may be shaped into bottles, vases, marbles, and other things. Glass is made from sand, limestone rock, and a material called sodium carbonate that is dug out of the earth.

Glass is not a new material like plastic. It has been made for thousands of years. Today, it is usually made in a factory called a glassworks.

How glass bottles are made

❶ Pieces of crushed sand, limestone, and sodium carbonate are mixed together and melted in a hot oven.

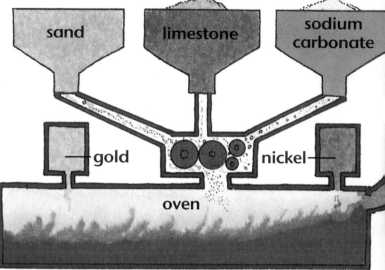

❷ To make colored glass, metals are added. For example, nickel makes the glass yellow and gold makes it red.

▲ This roller is smoothing out melted glass into a sheet. The sheet will then be floated over a layer of melted tin to make it perfectly flat. Glass that is made like this is used for windows and doors.

Did you know?

Sometimes glass is made when lightning strikes a sandy beach. The heat from the lightning melts the sand and other rocks, and they mix together.

Crystal is glass that sparkles. It sparkles because the metal called lead has been added to it.

Threads of **fiberglass** are smaller than human hairs.

▶ This girl's baseball has broken the window. Broken glass is sharp, so ask an adult to clear it up.

3 The red-hot, runny glass is dropped down a tube into iron molds that travel along a track.

air

mold

glass

oven

bottle cooling

4 Air is blown down the tubes into the molds, so that the glass cools and takes on the shape of the molds.

Reusing glass

In some places, glass bottles are used for milk, and soda. The bottles are washed and used over and over again. This saves the cost of making new bottles and makes less trash.

Even if a bottle can't be reused, it can be **recycled**. People bring their old bottles to collection centers. The bottles are cleaned, crushed, and melted to make new containers.

5 The bottles are heated up and cooled again to make the glass strong. Then they are taken away to be used.

Blowing glass by hand

Before **machines** were invented, glass bottles were made by hand. People blew air down a tube into liquid glass. Only expensive glass is made this way today.

45

Guitar

A guitar is a stringed musical instrument. Its body is made of light wood, such as pine, redwood, or walnut. It is hollow inside and has a sound hole, and a long, thin neck. Usually, six strings made of nylon or steel are stretched along the length of a guitar. They can be made tighter or looser by turning pegs at the top of the neck. Sounds are made by plucking or strumming the strings.

peg head

tuning peg

fret

neck

string

finger board

sound hole

bridge

sound board

Sound from string

1 If you pluck a guitar string, it **vibrates** (vy-BRAYTS) very quickly.

2 The vibrating string shakes the air around it. The shaking reaches your ears as a sound.

3 The hollow body of the guitar vibrates with the string and makes the sound louder.

4 A shorter string makes a higher sound. Pressing down on a string while you pluck it makes the sound higher.

Electric guitars

Electric guitars are **solid** and do not have a sound hole. When you pluck the strings, you send electrical signals to an amplifier (AMP-li-fy-er). This makes the signals louder. Then the signals go to a speaker that changes them into sounds.

▲ An electric guitar can be made louder than an ordinary guitar, and produces a lot more different sounds.

now picture this

The largest guitar in the world was made in Indiana in 1991. The guitar is over 38 feet long (almost as long as two limousines) and needs six people to play it.

See also Building, Fire, Store; ALL ABOUT PEOPLE Eating

Kitchen

▼ The chef, or cook, in a large restaurant needs a lot of cooking equipment.

A kitchen is a room where people store and cook food, wash dirty dishes, and keep all kinds of cooking and eating equipment, such as pots, pans, knives, bowls, and plates.

Did you know?

Food was first stored in airtight cans in 1810, but the first can-opener was not invented until 40 years later.

In the Food Museum in Switzerland, there is a small honey and sesame (SESS-a-mee) cake that is thought to be nearly 4,200 years old. It was sealed in an airtight container inside an ancient Egyptian tomb.

Storing food

Fresh food does not last for more than a few days. After a week or two in the air, a fresh apple turns brown and starts to rot.

Dried foods, such as raisins, stay fresh for months. In space, astronauts use food that is dried as a powder. They add water to their food in order to eat it.

Food that is sealed inside an airtight can lasts for several years.

Food spoils quickest when it is warm. Keeping food cold in a refrigerator helps it to last a few days longer.

A freezer makes all the liquid inside food turn into ice. Frozen food lasts for up to one year.

Keeping clean

It is very important to keep a kitchen or cooking area clean. Cleaning kills **germs** that live and grow in dirty places. Be sure to wash your hands and your food before you cook it.

▶ Not everyone uses a kitchen. In many countries, people live in small homes and cook their food outside.

Light

Light is a kind of **energy** that we use in order to see. Stars and lamps make light, but the brightest light on earth comes from the sun. Sunlight comes to the earth all the time, even when the sky is cloudy. Without light, the earth would be pitch black, and nothing would be able to live and grow here. People once used candles or lanterns to provide light at night, but now we use electric light. The energy for electric lights is delivered through wires or by batteries.

▼ Sunlight seems to have no color, but when it shines through rain drops, the colors mixed together in sunlight are split into a rainbow.

NEVER LOOK STRAIGHT AT THE SUN, EVEN WITH SUNGLASSES ON. IT IS SO BRIGHT THAT IT COULD DAMAGE YOUR EYES.

▶ At night, runways and airplanes are lit up with electric lights to make flying as safe as possible.

Light at night

At night, as our part of the earth turns away from the sun, we lose its light. We switch on lights that are powered by electricity and carry on our work or play.

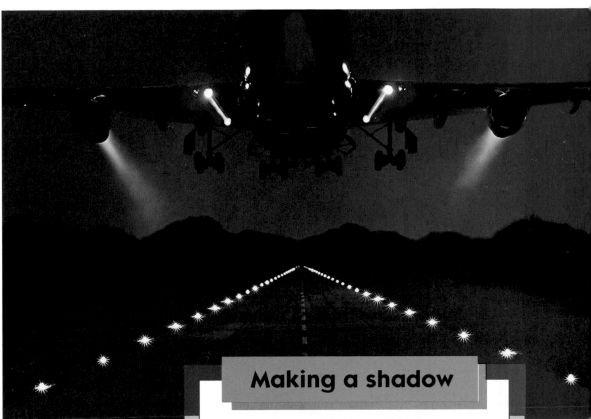

▼ Light from a **laser beam** is so powerful that it can be used to drill a hole through strong metal.

Making a shadow

Rays of light will shine through something clear, like glass, but when light hits something that isn't clear, such as your body, it can't shine through.

Your body blocks out the light and leaves a patch behind you where there is no light. This patch is called a shadow.

Metal

A metal is a **material** that is often hard and shiny, and can be bent into different shapes. Iron, steel, copper, and tin are all metals. Most metals are found in the earth. Some metals, such as gold and silver, can be dug out of the ground. Others, such as iron, are found as rocks called ores. The ore has to be heated to get the metal out.

▼ Gold can sometimes be found in rivers and streams. "Panning" is a way of separating gold from other metals.

▲ A lump of gold dug out of the earth is called a nugget.

Melting metals

When metals are heated, they soften and can be pressed into different shapes. Metals harden again as they grow cool.

◄ This metal worker is using a hot flame to weld, or join, pieces of metal together.

If metals are heated to very high **temperatures**, they melt into a liquid and can be mixed together like paints. Iron will mix with tiny amounts of other metals to make steel, one of the strongest building materials in the world. Steel is more useful than the metals it comes from.

▶ Sometimes metals are melted down and poured into special molds called bars, or ingots. This way they are easier to store.

World champion metal

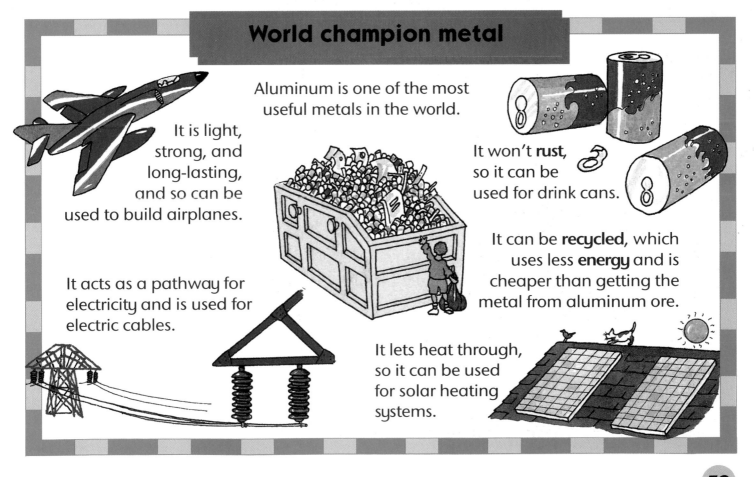

Aluminum is one of the most useful metals in the world.

It is light, strong, and long-lasting, and so can be used to build airplanes.

It won't **rust**, so it can be used for drink cans.

It can be **recycled**, which uses less **energy** and is cheaper than getting the metal from aluminum ore.

It acts as a pathway for electricity and is used for electric cables.

It lets heat through, so it can be used for solar heating systems.

See also Computer, Metal, Plastic, Store

Money

People use money to pay for the things they buy. Everyone needs some money to pay for services, such as heating and water, and to buy goods, such as food and clothes. Most people have to earn money by doing a job. For this, they are paid a **salary**.

Around the world

Every country in the world has its own kind of money, called its currency (CUR-en-see). Dollars, pounds, and yen are all currencies. When you visit another country, you have to change your money into the currency of that country before you can buy food or other goods from stores.

Did you know?

Checks do not have to be written on paper. In Britain, a man once wrote a check on the side of a cow, and the money was still paid out of his bank account.

In 1986 a Swiss bank brought out a machine that allowed wealthy customers to take out solid gold bars or gold coins from the bank vaults while the bank was closed.

Plastic cards

Many people use a plastic credit card to buy goods. Each card has a number written in code on a metal strip on the back. A **machine** at a checkout "reads" this number and links up with a computer at the customer's bank. The bank sends a bill to the customer once a month.

▲ In most countries, people use money to buy the things they need.

now picture this

The world's largest credit card wallet is 250 ft long and holds 1,356 cards. It would reach the ground from the top of a 30-story building.

The history of money

Before there was any money, people exchanged one kind of goods for another. People used shells, beans, and beads to buy food.

The first coins were made of gold or silver, so that the coins themselves were valuable.

Today, paper money and coins are not made of valuable **materials**, but they are still worth the amount which they have stamped or printed on them.

In the bank

Walking around with a lot of money or storing it in a box can be risky. It may be lost or stolen. Many people prefer to keep their money in a bank. The bank takes care of the money and gives people checks to buy goods. It uses computers to keep track of how much money its customers have left.

▲ Most banks have a safe made of strong steel where people's money can be kept secure.

Movie

A movie tells a story through sound and moving pictures. We can watch movies in a theater on a big screen, or on television. Movies usually begin as a script in which a writer tells a story. Then actors are chosen to play each character. Movies can be very exciting. Special effects can make you believe that animals talk English, or that people can make friends with beings from outer space.

Making a movie

Movies are made by movie companies. They often cost a lot of money. A movie company hires hundreds of people who work together to make the movie.

Did you know?

Walt Disney's famous mouse was first called Mortimer. He was renamed Mickey in 1928.

Hollywood's important Oscar awards are not just given to adults. In 1994, at the age of 11, Anna Paquin won an Oscar for her part in the film *The Piano*.

One hour of a movie uses up around 4,020 ft of film.

❸ Much of the movie is filmed in a **studio**. Painters and set builders can make a studio look like the planet Mars or a street in the Wild West.

❶ The director is in charge of the filming. He or she decides how every part of the movie should look, and how the actors should perform.

❷ Actors learn the words of the script and rehearse their parts before filming begins.

Cartoons

Cartoons are made by filming thousands of drawings for a split second each.

The drawings are all a little different from each other. When they are shown very quickly one after another, as a movie, it looks as if they are moving on the screen.

4 Sometimes stunt men and women perform dangerous stunts in the movie. They practice hard before filming begins.

5 **Engineers** control the lighting on set, record the sound track, and operate the cameras.

6 After filming, the film editor takes the best parts of the movie, and joins them together in a movie of the right length.

▶ Anyone who has a video recorder or movie camera can make movies.

57

See also Book, Office, Store

Museum

A museum is a building that displays interesting, unusual, and often very old objects. Visitors come to the museum to see the objects, and learn from them. Most museums collect objects of a certain kind, such as paintings, spacecraft, or things from other **cultures**. Some even collect toys.

Inside a museum

Some displays let people find out what it is like to do a job, for example to drive a train or fly a spacecraft.

Some visitors hire a guidebook and a tape that tell them about the displays.

There is often a shop that sells books and pictures or models of the displays.

Museum guides show visitors around the displays.

Visitors pay to enter the museum.

Some museums have rooms where younger visitors can make models of the things on display in different parts of the museum.

Most museums have a cafeteria where visitors can eat and drink.

The museum has offices where the people who run the museum work.

All museums have an area where objects are cleaned and repaired.

Some museums have exciting displays that visitors can make work for themselves.

In the museum library, people can look up information about different objects or people.

Curators are experts. They give talks about their displays, buy new objects, and arrange new displays for them.

Office

An office is a place where people plan, organize, and carry out their work. It is like a control center. Modern offices usually have lots of **machines** that make this work easier. All businesses, as well as hospitals, stores, and factories, have an office. Schools have offices too, where workers help the principal run the school. They greet visitors to the school, help students, keep records of grades and attendance, and write letters to parents and staff.

A school office

Personal computers may be used for writing letters and reports, for keeping track of numbers in classes, and for sorting lists of names.

Important information, about students and staff for example, is kept in a filing cabinet as well as in the computer.

A calculator helps do math quickly.

A telephone allows people in different places to talk to each other. If a student becomes ill, the secretary may call his or her family.

Photocopiers can copy letters in seconds. They can make 100 copies in less than one minute.

A fax machine can copy a sheet of paper, such as an order for more textbooks, and send it by telephone line to another fax machine in seconds.

An answering machine uses a tape to record messages from people who phone the office when no one is there.

61

Oil

Oil is a dark, thick liquid which lies deep inside the earth. It was formed from tiny plants and animals that once lived in the sea. As they died, they sank to the bottom and were buried in mud. Over the years, the mud changed into hard, heavy rock.

The rock slowly pushed down on the rotting plants and animals, and changed them into the black, sticky **material** which we call oil. Finding oil and getting it out of the ground is hard work, and expensive. It's worth the effort because oil is so useful.

derrick

drill pipe

mud hose

mud and soil

An oil well

Oil collects in holes inside rocks deep down in the earth. Oil companies use a drill bit on the end of a long pipe to dig down to the oil. During drilling they pump mud down the pipe to cool the bit and push soil out of the pipe and back up to the surface. When they reach the oil, they line the well with a strong steel pipe. The oil flows to the surface along tubes inside the pipe.

drill bit

gas

oil

water

At the refinery

When oil reaches the surface, it is piped to a factory called an oil refinery. Here it is heated until it separates into different kinds of oil. Light oils are used as **fuel** for **vehicles** (VEE-hic-els) and electricity **generators** (JEN-er-ay-tors). Thicker oils are used to keep moving parts inside **machines** running smoothly.

▶ Oil rigs are built at sea to pump oil from the seabed. Rigs are usually so far from land that the workers are flown in by helicopter.

How is oil used?

Oil is used to make electricity. It is burned to heat water to make the steam that drives electricity generators.

Tar that is used to cover roads is made from oil.

Oil is used to make nylon and other clothes fabrics.

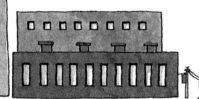

Oil is used in plastic and polyethylene (pol-EE-thi-leen) goods.

Oil is used for gasoline and **diesel** (DEE-zel) fuel for cars, buses, tractors, trucks, and some trains.

People are trying to find new ways of making these things because the world's supplies of oil are running out.

Plastic

Plastic is a factory-made **material** that can be molded into different shapes. It was first made in the United States about 90 years ago. Plastic is light but strong, and can be bright and colorful. It is very useful because it doesn't fall apart easily, or **rust** in the open air. Often plastic is used to make things that used to be made from natural materials, such as wood or metal.

▶ Plastic is stored as grains. The grains are melted down later on and poured into molds.

Why plastic?

Hard plastics are used to make chairs and crash helmets.

Soft plastics are used to make shower curtains and trash bags.

Plastic is used to strengthen other materials, such as **fabric** for clothes.

Plastic is easy to clean and hard to break. It is used for food packaging and to make plates, knives, and forks used for picnics.

Plastic is not harmed by rain or snow, so it is used to make telephone booths.

Recycling plastic

Because plastic doesn't break down easily, it takes up lots of space in landfills when people throw it away. One answer to this problem is for people to **recycle** plastic. Plastics are collected at recycling centers and taken to factories. Here they are melted down to make new things, such as flower pots and trash cans. Other people are trying to make plastic that will break down when it is thrown away.

▶ Before recycling, plastic objects must be sorted into soft and hard plastics. Different kinds of plastic are recycled in different ways.

Did you know?

The black lining inside a nonstick saucepan is a kind of plastic.

Perspex is a strong, clear plastic. It is used to build see-through squash courts for squash matches so that as many people as possible can watch.

Plastic surgeons are named after the supple or "plastic" skin that they mold.

Plastic in surgery

Some kinds of plastics are safe to use inside the human body. When people break their bones in an accident, the broken bones may be joined together again by plastic screws and pins. Surgeons use different plastics for the thread they use to sew up wounds, and to replace damaged parts of organs such as the heart.

Radio

A radio is a **machine** that sends and receives electrical signals by radio waves. Most people use radios to listen to music, news, and other programs **broadcast** from a radio station. However, two-way radios also allow people in different places to talk directly to each other. Two-way radios are often used by the armed forces, as well as by train, bus, and cab companies, to keep people in touch with each other.

▲ Sports commentators use radio headsets to keep in touch with the people at the television studio.

A radio broadcast

Radios send out messages by using invisible signals called radio waves. The signals are silent until they reach another radio which can turn them into sounds.

❷ The electrical signals travel along a wire to a transmitter.

❶ At a radio station, disc jockeys and newsreaders sit in a **studio** to broadcast a program. Their voices create **vibrations** (vy-BRAY-shuns) in the air. The microphone changes the vibrations into electrical signals.

3 The transmitter changes the electrical signals into radio waves. The waves travel through the air, hundreds of miles away from the transmitter.

4 In less than a second, the waves reach your radio **aerial** (AIR-ee-al), which changes the waves back into electrical signals.

5 The signals pass down the aerial to your radio. Inside your radio the speaker turns the signals back into sounds that your ears can hear.

Keeping in touch

Radio waves can be used to keep ships at sea in contact with their port, and astronauts in space in touch with the earth. Radios help to keep people safe. Police officers carry radios with them to talk to the police station or call other officers for help.

▲ Inuit (IN-oo-it) hunters in remote areas of Canada keep in touch with other camps and settlements by radio.

◀ If an athlete is injured, medical staff can radio quickly for a stretcher or ambulance.

Robot

A robot is a **machine** that can be used instead of a person to do a job. Most robots are controlled by computers. Many robots are moving arms that do not have bodies. They are often used in factories to make **mass-produced** goods. Robots are also used for dangerous jobs. If the police find a bomb, a robot may be used to defuse it.

Building cars

Robots are used to do the simple jobs needed to build cars. The cars move along a track between the robots as they work.

1 Robots tighten the screws in the doors of the cars.

2 Robots **weld** the same sheets of metal together on each car.

3 Robots spray the body of the cars with paint.

Robots do these jobs quickly and perfectly. They never get tired, but their parts do wear out.

Did you know?

A robot sheep-shearer has been invented in Australia. The robot can shear a sheep in just 100 seconds, more than one minute faster than a human shearer can.

In Japan, some places do not have enough Shinto priests for all the **shrines**. Some shrines are now using robots to chant prayers instead of priests.

▶ Some robots have to hold small or delicate objects. This robot "hand" is being tested for its grip.

Under the sea

In 1986, divers used a robot called Jason Junior to explore the wreck of the ocean liner Titanic. The wreck lay on the seabed $2\frac{1}{2}$ miles below the surface of the sea.

Jason Junior carried two cameras that took pictures of the Titanic. Jason Junior was attached by a cable to a submarine, and the submarine's crew controlled it from there by computer.

▲ This robot helps to collect money for the Leslie Frost Natural Resources Centre in Ontario, Canada.

Roller coaster

A roller coaster is a ride at an amusement park. Its cars run along a track. The track goes up and down and around sharp curves. Sometimes it loops upside down. A roller coaster has no engine. Instead, invisible **forces** make the cars speed up and slow down.

Gravity

The force that tugs everything towards the middle of the earth is called **gravity**. It is gravity that makes something you have dropped fall to the ground. You cannot feel gravity, but it also keeps you on the surface of the earth, no matter where in the world you are.

Into action

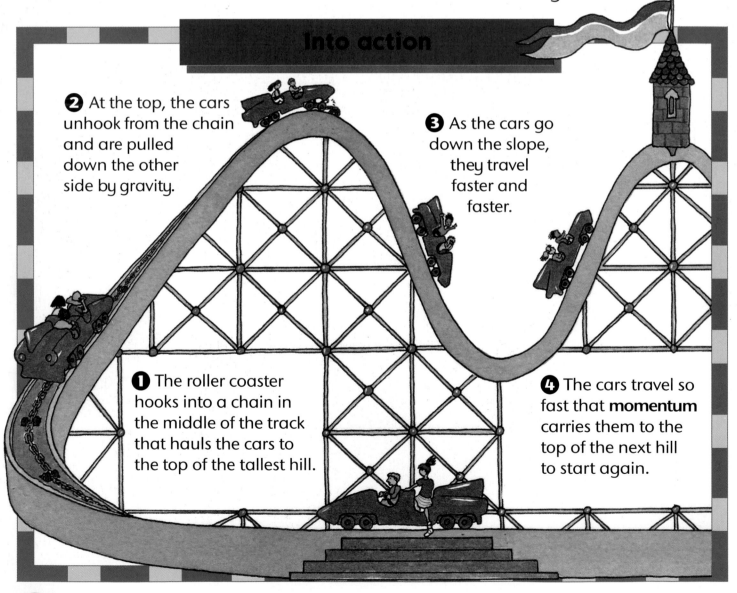

❷ At the top, the cars unhook from the chain and are pulled down the other side by gravity.

❸ As the cars go down the slope, they travel faster and faster.

❶ The roller coaster hooks into a chain in the middle of the track that hauls the cars to the top of the tallest hill.

❹ The cars travel so fast that **momentum** carries them to the top of the next hill to start again.

When a roller coaster loops the loop, the passengers feel pushed back into their seats. This is because momentum keeps their bodies traveling upward for a short time as the cars start to come down.

▼ Even if a roller coaster in a loop had no outside wheels to grip the track, it would not fall off the track as long as it was traveling fast enough.

Space shuttle

A space shuttle is a spacecraft that can fly into space again and again. It may take new **satellites** into space, or repair ones already there. Sometimes it carries astronauts who perform scientific experiments. The shuttle has two parts, one for the astronauts, and another made up of the booster rockets and **fuel** tank. Both parts of the shuttle can be reused. This makes the space shuttle different from spacecraft that can only make one flight.

A shuttle mission

4 The shuttle's smaller engines guide it into **orbit**. **Gravity** keeps it circling the earth until its mission is over.

3 Nine minutes later the fuel tank is empty and drops away.

1 On the launch pad, the shuttle's booster rockets fire and begin to burn fuel. The shuttle lifts off.

2 Two minutes later, the boosters have run out of fuel. They fall into the sea.

The boosters are fished out of the sea to be used again.

5 When it has finished its mission, the shuttle's engines slow the shuttle down and steer it back towards the earth.

6 The shuttle is pulled down faster towards the earth by gravity.

7 The shuttle enters the earth's **atmosphere** (AT-moss-fear). As it pushes through the air, **friction** (FRICK-shun) makes the shuttle heat up and glow red-hot.

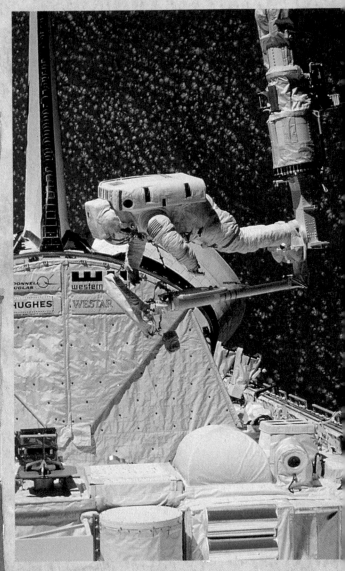

▲ Astronauts can be fixed to the robotic arm in the cargo bay to help them inspect the shuttle's cargo.

8 The shuttle glides down without engine **power** and lands on an ordinary runway.

Store

A store is a place where goods are sold. For example, a supermarket sells food and drinks. Some stores sell one kind of thing, others may sell many. Often stores are self-service. This means that you walk around the store, putting all the things you need in a shopping cart. Before leaving the store, you pay for your goods at the checkout counter.

Inside a supermarket

In the office, people hire staff and pay them, take care of all the money, order new deliveries and make sure they arrive.

The in-store bakery makes fresh bread, muffins, and desserts to sell in the store.

Goods are stored in the stockroom.

Trucks bring goods to the store. The drivers park in the delivery area to unload.

Clerks at the deli counter serve customers with cheeses, cold meats, and fresh salads.

The manager is the person in charge of the store.

Some workers fill the shelves with goods from the stock room.

At the checkout counter the bar codes, or black lines that record the price of each item, are "read" by a **laser beam**. The cash register adds up all the prices, tells the cashier how much change to give the customer, and prints a receipt (re-SEET).

Automatic doors open when people walk on a special mat in front of the door. They close behind people when they leave.

Most stores have a parking lot so that customers can wheel their groceries straight to the car.

Telephone

A telephone is an electrical **machine** that is used to talk to people in another place. The sound of a person's voice doesn't travel very far on its own. A telephone uses electricity to change the voice into signals that flash along electrical cables, or cables made of **optical fiber**, to a telephone in another street or another country, all in a few seconds. Cordless telephones act like two-way radios. They change your voice into radio waves that travel to another telephone through the air.

A long-distance call

1 As you press the numbers on your telephone, they are changed into electrical signals.

3 The telephone exchange changes the light signals into radio waves. The waves are beamed into space by a transmitter.

2 Your telephone changes the electrical signals into flashes of light that travel along optical fiber cables to the telephone exchange.

4 A **satellite** in space receives the waves and beams them back to a telephone exchange in another country.

5 Your friend's telephone receives the waves from the telephone exchange and rings.

6 When your friend speaks, his or her voice is changed into signals which travel back along the same route to your telephone.

Optical fiber

Inside an optical fiber, light flashes backward and forward across the fiber. This allows signals to travel around bends. Modern telephones use optical fibers because light travels faster than electricity and the fibers carry more signals than electrical wires can.

light

▲ Optical fibers inside a cable are made of glass or plastic and are the width of a human hair.

Television

A television is a **machine** that uses radio waves to make moving pictures appear on a screen in the television set and to send sounds to the speakers. Many people in the world have a television in their home. Many have more than one. Some people watch only the news. Others watch television all day. Today, television is one of the most important ways people learn about what is happening in the world.

A television broadcast

Around the world
Television companies use space **satellites** to send their programs around the world. They send radio waves up to a satellite, which then bounces them down to receivers on the ground. Then people around the world can sit comfortably at home and watch events in other countries, such as the Olympic Games, as they are taking place.

❶ At the television **studio**, cameras change the images they "see" into electrical picture signals. Microphones change sound **vibrations** (vy-BRAY-shuns) into electrical sound signals.

❷ The picture and sound signals travel along wires to a transmitter. The transmitter changes the signals into radio waves and sends them through the air.

Video recording

Once radio waves have been changed into electrical signals, they can be saved as patterns on magnetic video tape. This allows people to record programs and play them back through their television sets whenever they want.

▶ Camera operators may sometimes use monitors to see which camera's signals are being broadcast.

5 The sound signals travel to the speaker where they are changed back into sounds.

3 In less than a second, a home television **aerial** (AIR-ee-al) picks up the radio waves. It changes them back into electrical signals.

4 The signals flow along wires into the television set. The picture signals are used to light up dots on the television screen to make the color pictures.

Tractor

A tractor is a motor **vehicle** (VEE-hic-el) with large wheels, and a powerful **diesel** (DEE-zel) engine. Tractors were invented about 100 years ago. They pull heavy loads and machinery on farms, such as plows and seed drills. Tractors work faster than animals and do not get tired. In one day a tractor can plow as many fields as a horse-drawn plow could work in one week.

How a tractor works

A tractor's engine is bigger and more powerful than a car's, but it is cheaper to run. Diesel oil costs less than gasoline, and diesel engines need less **fuel** to work.

The exhaust (ig-ZOST) pipe takes waste **fumes** out of the engine.

The brake drums slow the wheels down so that they stop.

The driver's cab is high up to give a good view.

The steering wheel changes the direction of the front wheels.

The engine burns fuel and gives the tractor the **power** to move.

The rear wheels give the tractor a good grip on muddy ground.

The transmission (trans-MISH-un) gives the wheels the right amount of power for the job they have to do.

A machine for all seasons

Farmers use tractors to pull different pieces of machinery at different times of the year.

In spring, a plow breaks up the soil for planting seeds. A seed drill puts the right amount of seed into the plowed soil. It covers the seeds over so that birds don't eat them.

In summer, a sprayer soaks the growing crops with a spray that kills pests.

In the fall, the tractor works alongside a combine harvester to gather in the harvested crops.

Getting a grip
Tractors have to work where there is a lot of mud. To stop them from getting stuck, the huge wheels on a tractor have thick tires with a deep **tread**. The grooves in the tread let muddy water escape and help the tire to grip the ground beneath.

The front wheels guide the tractor in the right direction.

▲ Oil makes the engine work smoothly by reducing **friction** (FRICK-shun).

81

Train

A train is a line of cars pulled by an engine along a railroad track. Trains are used to transport both goods and people. The first trains were invented about 150 years ago and were pulled by steam engines. Most modern trains run on **diesel** (DEE-zel) oil or electricity.

▶ Trains can travel in all sorts of weather. In high-up places, snow plows fixed to the front of engines clear snow off the tracks.

A modern train

The front of the engine is rounded in shape so that it can push through the air more easily.

The driver's cab has an instrument panel and a radio. The radio allows the driver to talk to the signal operators who control all the trains on the line. If there is an accident further up the line, the signal operators can warn the driver to stop.

Air-conditioning keeps the cars cool in hot weather. A heating system keeps them warm when the weather is cold.

Trains and the environment

Trains may be the best form of transportation in the future. A train can carry a heavier load than a truck or bus, and uses less **fuel**. This helps to keep the **environment** clean. By keeping heavy trucks off the roads, trains also make them quieter, and safer for other drivers to use.

▶ To make room for roads and walkways, some cities have railroad tracks that go overhead or run underground.

Modern electric trains often run on electricity that comes from cables overhead. Electric trains do not need a fuel tank, so they weigh less and travel faster than diesel trains.

Keeping track

Trains have smooth metal wheels that have a sloping edge. This shape keeps the wheels on the track around bends. A rim, or flange, on the inside of each wheel keeps it on the track around very tight bends.

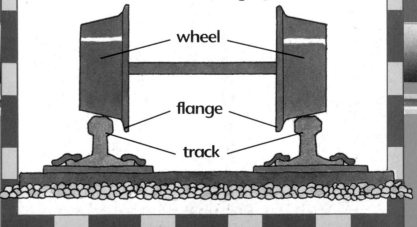

wheel

flange

track

Truck

A truck is a large, powerful road **vehicle** (VEE-hic-el) that is used to carry goods from one place to another. Trucks are designed and built to do different jobs. The simplest kinds of trucks take groceries to stores. A huge logging truck can load whole tree trunks on its trailer and haul them down from a forest to a timber yard.

▲ Dump trucks have an arm that tips up the trailer to unload their cargo.

A refrigerated truck

The air deflector helps air flow smoothly over the top of the truck so that it can go faster.

The cab is where the driver rides.

The truck's **diesel** (DEE-zel) engine can pull heavy loads.

Double wheels spread the load over a wide surface, and keep the truck steady if a tire blows out.

The **fuel** tank stores diesel oil.

▶ In Australia there are huge road trains. Each truck can pull up to three trailers at a time.

The refrigerated trailer keeps the load of food or drinks inside it cool.

Working in pairs

Most big trucks are articulated (ar-TIK-you-lay-ted). This means they are built in more than one piece. They have an engine in front and at least one trailer behind.

This design allows the truck to turn corners more tightly than it could if it were built in one piece.

Wheel

A wheel is a circle of strong **material** fixed around a center axle (AX-el). The wheel was invented about 5,000 years ago. People found that it was much easier to carry goods around in a cart with wheels than it was to drag them along the ground. The wheel is a simple but important invention that is used in almost all modern forms of transportation.

Wheels for speed

The first wheels were **solid**, but most solid wheels are heavy and slow a **vehicle** (VEE-hic-el) down. Spokes make wheels lighter so that vehicles can reach fast speeds more quickly.

Wheels at work

An object sliding along the ground rubs against the ground and is slowed down by **friction** (FRICK-shun).

friction

friction

As a wheel turns, the part touching the ground is always changing. There is very little rubbing against the ground, and less friction.

▲ Motorbike wheels are light and can travel very fast.

▶ The Ferris wheel at an amusement park is made with spokes so that it is strong, but light, and will not collapse.

Axles and bearings

Wheels are attached to vehicles by metal bars called axles. To stop a wheel rubbing against its axle and being slowed down by friction, the bar is surrounded by a ring of shiny, metal bearings. Bearings can be shaped like balls, rollers, or needles. As the wheel and axle turn, the bearings turn around, cutting down on friction.

Wheels on an In-line skate

rubber tire

ball bearing

axle

Glossary

Aerial Something that gives out or picks up radio waves that travel through the air.

Atmosphere The layer of air and other gases that surround the earth.

Bound Something stuck or sewn together.

Broadcast Sent out by radio waves through the air.

Culture The ideas, crafts, and customs of different countries or peoples.

Diesel A thick, heavy fuel made from oil.

Distribution warehouse The place where goods are kept before going to a store.

Efficient Something that works without wasting too much energy.

Energy What makes people and machines able to do work. Energy comes from things such as fuels, the sun, water, or wind.

Engineer Someone who plans, builds, or looks after things such as machines, engines, roads, and bridges.

Environment The world around you.

Fabric Cloth used for making things such as clothes, and for covering furniture.

Fiberglass A material that is made of glass threads.

Filter A thing like a sieve that allows some materials through and keeps others out.

Force A push or pull that changes the way an object moves or starts it moving.

Friction The rubbing of things against each other that slows them down.

Fuel Something that gives out energy as heat or power when it burns.

Fumes Smoke, gas, or vapor that is often irritating.

Generator A machine that changes mechanical energy into electrical energy.

Germ A tiny living thing that can make people and animals sick.

Gravity The force that pulls things into the center of the earth. Gravity also pulls the planets toward the sun.

Laser beam A very narrow, powerful ray of light that can cut through hard materials.

Lens A curved piece of glass or plastic that bends light.

Machine A device with moving parts that work together to do a job.

Mass produce To make something in large numbers. This way of making things is called mass production.

Material The thing an object is made from.

Momentum The force that makes a moving object keep going in the same direction.

Negative A picture on photographic film that shows shadows as light areas and light areas as dark patches.

Nuclear energy A kind of energy that is produced when particles of uranium metal are split in two.

Optical fiber A thin thread of plastic or glass that lets rays of light travel along inside it.

Orbit The curved path of a planet, moon, or spacecraft around a planet or star.

Power The strength to do a job.

Power shovel A machine that builders use to dig up large amounts of soil.

Power station A large factory where generators make electricity.

Propeller Something that has blades fixed to a center hub and moves a ship or airplane forward when it turns.

Radar A way of tracking ships or airplanes by sending out radio waves. Waves that hit an object bounce back and are picked up by a receiver.

Ray Light that is traveling in a straight line.

Recycle To use an object or material to make something else.

Rust When iron or steel turns brown and breaks up in damp air.

Salary Money paid to someone each month in return for work.

Satellite Something that circles planets. People make machines called satellites in order to send signals from one country to another or to take photographs of the earth.

Shrine A place where people pay respect to gods or saints.

Solid Something that is made in one piece and has a set shape and size.

Source A place where things come from.

Streamlined Something that is smooth and even so that it can move quickly without wasting much energy.

Studio A place where people make movies, records, or programs for radio or television.

Temperature A level of heat. Your temperature is how hot you are.

Treatment plant A factory for cleaning water.

Vehicle A machine that is used to carry people or goods.

Vibrate To move backward and forward very fast. The movements are called vibrations.

Weld To join pieces of metal by melting and pressing them together so that they cool in one piece.

Index

A

aerial *67, 79*
air-conditioning *82*
air deflector 84
airplane *12-13, 51, 53*
airport 13
aluminum 13, 19, 53
amplifier 46
Anna Paquin 56
answering machine 61
aperture 28
arched bridge *22*
architect 24
articulated truck *85*
artist 56
astronaut *67, 72*
atmosphere 73
atomic clock 34
Australia *69, 85*
automatic door 26, 75
axle 86, *87*

B

bakery 74
bank *54, 55*
bar code 75
bathroom 14-15, 25, 33
bathtub 14
beam bridge *22*
bearing *87*
bike *16-17, 18, 40, 41*
boat *18*-19
Boeing 747 13
book 20-21, 58
booster rocket *72*
brake *17, 30, 40, 80*
brake drum 30, 80
brake pedal 30

brick 25
bricklayer 25
bridge *22*-23
Britain 54
broadcasting 66-67, 78-79
bubble bath 15
builder 24, 25
building 23, *24-25*
buildings *32-33, 40, 58*
bus *26-27, 33*, 83

C

cable *22, 24, 27, 33, 38,
    39, 53, 69, 76, 83*
cafeteria 59
calculator *9*, 60
camera *28-29, 57, 69,
    78, 79*
Canada 67
car 26, *30-31, 40*, 68
cargo 13, 73
carpenter 25
cartoon *57*
cement 24, 25
cement mixer 25
cesspool 14
chain 16
check 55
chef 48
circuit 38
city 32-33
clock *34-35*
clothing 40, 63, 64
coin 55
computer *21, 36-37, 54,
    55*, 60, 69
computer scanner 36
concrete 23

cooking 42, 48, 49
copper 52
cordless telephone 76, *77*
credit card 54
curator 59

D

deli 75
delivery area 74
derrick 62
detergent 15
diesel oil 63, 80, 82, 84
digital clock 34
director 56
disk drive 36
disk jockey 66
distribution 41
diving watch 34
drain 32
dried food 49
drill bit 62
drill pipe 62
drink can *53*
driver's cab 80, 82, 84
dump truck 24, 84

E

Earth 50, 62, 70, *72, 73*
egg timer *35*
electrical signal 66, 67, 76,
    77, 78, 79
electricity 11, 24, 27, 31, 32,
    33, 38-39, 46, 47, 50, 51,
    53, 63, 66, 67, 76-77, 79,
    82, 83
electricity generator 63
encyclopedia 21

energy 10, 11, 16, 19, 30, 31, 38, 39, 50
engine 12, 19, 26, 30, 72, 73, *80*, 81, 82, *84*
engineer 13, 23, 31, 37, 57
England 22
environment 17, 39, 83
exhaust *30*, 31, *80*

F

factory 9, 40-41, 42, 44, 60, 63, 65, 68
faucet 14, 33
fax machine 61
Ferris wheel 87
ferry *18*
fiberglass 19, 44
fiction 21
filing cabinet 60
film *28, 29*, 56
film editor 57
filter 31
finger board 46
fire 42-43
firefighter 43
firework 42
flange 83
flint 42
floating 18, 19
floorboard 25
floppy disk 36, 37
flower pot 65
flying 12
food 48, 49, 54, 74
food can 48, 49, 53
Food Museum, Switzerland 48
force 11, 12, 16, 19, 30, 39, 70

foundation 24
freezer 49
fret 46
friction 73, *86*, 87
fuel 10, 12, 13, 19, 31, 38, 42, 63, 72, 80, 82, 83
fuel tank *72*, 83, *84*
fumes 30, 31, 80

G

gas pipe 32
gasoline 30, 31, 63
gear *16*, 30, 40
generator 10, 38, 39, 63
germ 15, 49
glass 44-45, 77
gold 52, 54, 55
gravity 70, 72, 73
guidebook 58
guitar 46-47

H

handlebar 17
hard disk 37
headlight 31
health 14
heat 38, 42, 52, 53, 63
heating 54, 82
helicopter 63
Hollywood 56
hot-air balloon 42
hourglass *35*
house *24, 25*
Humber River 22

I

ignition 30
Inuit people 67
iron 45, 52

J

Japan 69
Jason Junior *69*
jet engine 12

K

keyboard 36
kiln 42
kitchen 25, 33, *48-49*

L

lamp 50
landfill 65
laser beam *21*, 51, 75
launch pad 72
lead crystal 44
lens 28
library 21, 59
light 38, 39, 42, 50-51, 76, 77
lightning 38, 44
limestone 44
liquid 62
logging truck 84

M

machine 8-9, 10-11, 12, 21, 28, 36, 38, 40-41, 45, 63, 66, 68, 76, 78, 81
manager 75
mass production 40, 68
material 13, 19, 23, 38, 40, 44, 52-53, 55, 62, 64-65, 86
melting 53, 64, 65
metal 19, 52-53, 83
metal ore 52
Mickey Mouse 56
microphone *66, 78*

mold 45, 53, 64
momentum *70*, 71
money 54-55, 56
movie *56-57*
movie camera 28, 29
motorbike 86
mouse 37
mud 62, *80*, 81
mud hose 62
museum 32, 33, 58-59
music 46

N

negative 29
newsreader 66
nickel 44
nugget 52
nylon 63

O

oar 19
off-road vehicle 31
office 59, 60-61
oil 62-63, 81
oil refinery 63
oil rig 63
oil tanker *18*
Olympic Games 78
optical fiber 76, *77*
orbit 72
Oscar award 56

P

paper 20, 21, 55
parking lot 75
peg head 46
personal computer 36
Perspex 65
photocopier 61
photograph 28-*29*
piping *14-15*, *25*, 32, 33

plasterer 25
plastic 54, 63, 64-65, 77
plastic surgeon 65
plow 80, 81
plumber 25
police 37, 67, 68
pollution 31
polyethylene 63
power 30, 73, 80
power station *38*, 39
principal 60
printer 37
printing 20, 21
propeller 19
publisher 20
pumping station 14

R

radar 13
radio *27*, 66-67, 82
radio waves 66, 76, 78, 79
raft 18
railroad 26, 82, 83
rainbow 50
receipt 75
recycling 45, 53, 65
refrigerated food 49, 85
refrigerated truck *84-85*
restaurant 32
road train 85
robot 40, 41, *68-69*, 73
robot hand 69
robotic arm 73
rock 52, 62
roller coaster *70*-71
Roman numerals 35
root bridge 23
rowboat *19*
rubber tire 87
runway 51, 73
rust 53, 64

S

safety rules 16, 39, 43, 45,
    50, 83
sailboat *19*
salary 54
sand 44
satellite 72, 73, *76*, 77, 78
saucepan 65
scaffolding 25
school office *60-61*
screen 36
script 56
secretary *60*
seed drill *80*
sewer 14, *15*, 32
shadow *51*
shampoo 15
ship 18, 19, 67
signal operator 82
silver 52, 55
sink 14
skyscraper 24, *33*
snow plow 82
soap 15
solar heating system *53*
solar-powered car 31
sound 46, 56, 57, 78, 79
sound board 46
sound hole 46
space shuttle *72-73*
speaker 67, 78, 79
spoke *16*, 41, 86, 87
star 50
"Stealth" bomber 13
steel 19, 23, 52, 53, 55
steering wheel 30, 80
stockroom 74
storage tower 14
store 32, 60, *74-75*, 84
storybook 20, 21

streamlining 12, 31
streetcar *27*, 33
studio *56, 78*
stunt *57*
submarine *69*
suburb 33
subway 26, *32*, 83
Sun 39, 50
sunlight 50
supermarket *74-75*
suspension bridge *22*

T

tar *63*
telephone 33, 60, *76-77*
telephone exchange *76, 77*
television 56, *78-79*
theater 33
ticket machine 27
time 34, 35
time zone 34
timetable 27
tin 52
tire *17*, 31, 80, *81*
Titanic 69
toilet 14, 33
track 70, 82, *83*
tractor *80*-81
train *82-83*
transmission 30, 80
transmitter 67, *76, 78*
transportation 12-13, 16-17,
   18-19, 26-27, 30-31, 72-73,
   82-83, 84-85, 86-87
tread *17*, 81
treatment plant *14, 15*
tripod *28*
truck 18, 74, 83, *84-85*
tuning peg 46
turn signal 31

two-way radio 66
typing 36, 60

U

underpass 33
underwater camera 29

V

vehicle 12-13, 16-17, 18-19,
   22, 26-27, 30-31, 63, 72-
   73, 80-81, 84-85, 86
viaduct 22
vibrations 46, 66, 78
video camera 28
video recording 79
viewfinder 28

W

Walt Disney 56
water 14-15, 33
water pipe 14, 33
welding 68
wheel 41, *80, 81, 83,*
   84, 86-87
wire 50
word processor 60
work 8, 9, 10, 11, 54, 60